WAKING UP
GRATEFUL

*Turning a Painful Past into
a Purposeful Present*

Pamela H. Say, BA,
MBA, CFRE

ISBN-13: 9781734998108

Cover design by: Pamela Say
Printed in the United States of America

"...during every stage of my medical training, whether I was studying surgery, cardiology, or pediatrics, it was obvious to me how the human organism works. When I began my psychiatric rotation, however, I was struck by the contrast between the incredible complexity of the mind and the ways that we human beings are connected and attached to one another, and how little psychiatrists knew about the origins of the problems they were treating. Would it be possible one day to know as much about brains, minds, and love as we do about the other systems that make up our organism?"

BESSEL VAN DER KOLK, M.D., THE BODY KEEPS THE SCORE

PART ONE: WHAT HAPPENED

The passionate pursuit to heal the human spirit is happening.

BROKEN PIECES

Three years and three months ago, at the milestone age of 40, I shattered.

It didn't happen out of nowhere, but to my psyche, that's exactly how it felt. I spent those first forty years startlingly dissociated from myself. I was like a thin glass vase teetering on the edge of the shelf for decades when I believed I was solidly planted on the ground.

My boyfriend Billy once told me there is a difference between denial and delusion. Denial would require a degree of awareness and the choice to reject it. It is an action. Delusion is a state of being. I was delusional.

Who is to say what finally created enough of a vibration that the vase, at long last, plummeted off the shelf, crashed hard on the tile floor, and exploded into a million tiny pieces. Looking back, I think there were many things.

A marriage that, on the surface, looked healthy but lacked any semblance of soul connection or communication. Working myself to the bone, full of tension, and managing the household. Never getting ahead or able to plan for the future. A relapse by someone I was absolutely codependent on. An undiagnosed teenager with autism I was desperate to help, but didn't know how. My father slowly dying before my eyes. My own drinking habit escalating.

It all played a part in my state of mind, but none of those circumstances initiated the collapse. It was always going to happen. It was inevitable, and it was put into motion the day I pulled the first breath into my lungs.

I choose to call my higher power God, so that's the word I'll use. We all have different belief systems so if you choose the universe, science, Allah, Mother Earth, your own spirit, or nothing except what IS – that's fine. For me, it's God.

I believe on that beautiful day in 1976, when my heart beat outside the womb for the very first time - when I sucked air into my lungs for the first time - I was perfectly me. I was exactly who God intended me to be. Inside my newborn heart and mind existed the potential for all my gifts to be realized – my creativity, passion, natural talents, and most of all, my love. This is how nearly every human comes into consciousness, I think. Then we are handed over to humans. We enter into the world.

For many of us, the divergent path starts quickly. In infancy, we hear fighting, startling noises, and things happen or are done to us. Even if you grow up in a safe house in a safe neighborhood and attend a safe school – unfair judgements may be placed on you through societal norms. A competitive nature often gets defined as poor sport. A sensitive nature is called weak and overly emotional. An energetic child is reprimanded until their unbridled energy gets all bottled up inside.

In my leadership trainings when I do strength assessments, adults are frequently shocked at the innate gifts and abilities revealed in their results. Those strengths were often the very behaviors they were criticized for as a child. As a result, they repressed them.

Yet, their strengths peaked through, even as they stifled them for fear of offending someone. I have seen so many trainees shed their old ideas and move on to do great things by realizing their gifts fully; by unbecoming what everyone else said they should be and becoming exactly who they are.

So it was for me. At 40 years old, some long-repressed part of me shouted loudly from deep inside, "Do you see me? I am here!" The path to recovery began.

RIGHTFUL QUESTIONING

I sat in the plastic seat at the school event. The off-white gymnasium illuminated from iridescent lighting. The principal stood behind the podium and spoke of the children's achievements. He was a humble, young man and delightfully ordinary. The students were in the first few rows and the rest of the seats were filled will parents, aunts, uncles, little brothers and sisters, and beaming grandparents.

One seat ahead on the other side, a bright, spirited little girl wriggled in her seat, playing with things. My daughter used to be that way but she heard every word you would say. The program was long, even for me, and I found my head getting heavy and my eyelids at half moon. The little girl asked questions of the man in the next seat. She stood up in her chair and hugged her mom's head. I could see it all out of the corner of my eye.

A woman a few seats over - perhaps an older Aunt or Grandmother – called the child to her with a curl of her finger, glaring. She reprimanded the child. As the program went on, this woman leaned forward time and again. She would stare at the little girl with the most awful look on her face – hoping to keep the child from making sounds and moving. I'm an adult and the woman's face bothered me. I watched the divergent path forming, right there in front of me.

Of course, as adults we have to teach children self-control. That's a given, but imagine if instead of stifling and shaming a highly energetic child, we challenged ourselves to hone that energy, lift it up, give it purpose, and celebrate the life in that little girl? Broadly in society, we rarely talk about ways to creatively address children's abilities – how we might make things a little less convenient for ourselves so we can develop their God-given gifts. Not only do we stifle and shame, but we label many of their gifts as disorders or disabilities because they don't fit with our systems and structures.

My daughter grew up with next-level ADHD. People reacted so harshly when it interrupted their plans. Had they engaged her in those plans she could have multiplied their energy and accomplished so much for them. A rare coach or teacher turned the practice or learning environment into a laboratory where kids of all abilities (not disabilities) were engaged, included and nurtured. It meant they had to plan a bit more, but it also meant the results were even greater!

In some cases, I didn't force my daughter to sit through hours-long events where there was nothing to do but listen. That would be torture so why make her, then shame her for it? When I had no choice, I resigned to the fact that those couple of hours would not be very enjoyable for me. Rather, I "worked" the event and my job was to keep my daughter engaged. I would pack a bag full of tricks, snacks, and quiet distractions. My attention would be on her; which allowed me to be present but also not expect her to be something she wasn't.

This example applies to many other abilities – like the super competitive child, the extremely sensitive child, the wildly analytical child, the very cerebral or artistic child, and all the other little God-made geniuses we're handed as a blank slate. But this book isn't about how you raise your kids. It's about you and it's about me.

When I witness shaming behavior, I wonder, how did those behaviors shape me? How did they turn into self-imposed ideas about who I should be? In what ways did they stifle my passion and creativity? Is that when I began to compare myself to others?

Judgements are critical to our early forming. It was those very kinds of behaviors that led my daughter with Autism to develop severe depression and anxiety, and not trust society. Thank God that is changing for her now.

For many, the rightful questioning rarely arises.

SET THEM FREE

I stood in the center of the living room in our house on the dead-end street where the factory used to be. It was the early 1990's. MTV played in the background. That year, Nirvana released Smells Like Teen Spirit. I never felt such feelings as I watched the scene of an alternate reality, where the sparkling clean world turned dark and foggy. It was like watching the world the way I saw it.

"I feel stupid and contagious…."

Was he talking to me?

My long, straight, unstyled blonde hair touched the middle of my back. I donned a blue flannel and ripped jeans. I never asked for much of anything – but for my birthday that year, I talked my parents into driving to the city. I had one stop to make - the underground record store. I got a Pearl Jam t-shirt and a tape of Rage Against the Machine with my own money.

Most people saw a surly, self-absorbed, rebellious teen. When I see kids like that, I see so much more.

Science tells us things. Reason can be trained as early as seven or eight. Those first eight years are critical to laying the foundation. Genes play a role but we are – if not equally – affected by the toxins introduced into our bodies, the people in our lives, and the environments around us. It's not nature or nurture; it's nature and nurture.

Chronic stress in children is known to be detrimental long-term; while play and exploration prove to be the very best foundation. So when we are stressing out about "getting it all right" for our children, we would best serve them by simply facilitating deliberate, healthy play.

To some people this will be heresy, but as a girl who grew up in a family wrought with mental health disorders, hospitalizations, and institutionalizations for generations, I wonder what "passing-down" really means. Is it the actual disorder we're genetically pre-disposed to? Yes. My daughter, for example, has autism. Perhaps, also, we are predisposed to behavior and that behavior exacerbates our nature.

To repeat and teach the traumatic stress of the generation before us disrupts healthy functioning. In that case, the corresponding brokenness becomes a spectrum of symptoms. Of course there are issues of brain chemistry, but those plus chronic stress can be a recipe for disaster.

As it turns out, science shows that chronic stress invades the tissues and can alter brain chemistry in a mother's infant child – meaning mom's stress affects the unborn baby. Whatever the case, I am sure some people are born wherein systems of the body and mind function abnormally – but that doesn't automatically equate, for example, to deviant behavior.

I have known people who spent years grappling with their diagnosis and no amount of treatment changed their symptoms, until they got to the heart of their traumatic stress, connected the dots of the past to the present, and reprocessed their memories.

Defiant teens are the greatest example of the need for more and better services around trauma processing. Around 12 years old we shift from concrete to complex thinking. This is also the age we begin to label our children "difficult and challenging," depicting them as disobedient and unruly. Adolescence is defined as ages 12 to 18. This is when human brains become capable of imagining possibilities, coming up with questions, debating long-taught ideas, and using logic to look at personal problems.

They will start to question the very authorities they blindly followed their whole lives – to decide what they believe is wrong or right. Ethics, goals, identity, world issues, competing views, plans and dreams – this is when it all begins. Why villainize that?

When I was a teenager I wanted to express that reasoning. The abuse I endured was something I started to question. I got shut down over and over in a variety of scenarios. Finally, right there, in the middle of the living room, I exploded. Screaming and crying, I pulled my own hair. I shouted, "I can't take it anymore."

My head throbbed as tears ran down my face. My behavior could be categorized as an "outburst." I was, in fact, labeled at-risk. I thought I was crazy and other people thought so too. I believed it so much, when I turned 24, I admitted myself to the psych ward. I needed to know what was wrong with me. Turns out, I just needed lots and lots of healing.

Today, you will never talk me out of my healthy defiance. Rediscovering my spirit is a beautiful invitation. I think of that little girl at the school event hugging her mom's head when I think of little Pammy – my child inside. I was a little girl who developed through early information. Was that information correct? Even spiritual texts point to something fascinating.

Jesus said, "Let the little children come to me, and do not hinder them, for the kingdom of Heaven belongs to such as these." You don't have to be a Christian or a religious person to see that children have the truest, closest connection to their spirit – if only we set them free.

Now, at 43, my resurrection comes by recovering my child within.

FINDING PAMMY

I sat on the couch in the therapist's office gripping my hands nervously and moving my thumbs about. Her office was in a nice building on a side street in a wealthy suburb. You could walk down the hall for colon hydrotherapy, a yoga class, or to get your brows done – a funny juxtaposition from the things being talked about in her room. It wasn't my scene but I loved my therapist. She wasn't just a listener; she was a problem solver like me.

She got to know me. A brilliant student of her field, she identified potential issues and brought in specialized tools and techniques. She systematically assessed and addressed my codependence, grief, dissociation, disorganized attachment, and Complex PTSD. When we hit a wall – and we did sometimes – she would reach out to colleagues with focused expertise and bring in new ideas to get me over the hump.

In about a year and a half we confronted a lifetime of trauma and effectively repositioned those experiences in my psyche. It laid a great foundation for a lifetime journey, as we undid a major portion of my early brain conditioning.

Miracles happened in that room with the light, bright walls; the tall bookshelf; the desk, couch and chair; the little round table with the dish full of candy; and her and me.

Pioneers. Explorers. Ghost Hunters. Truth Tellers. Reverse Psychics. Treasure Hunters. Spirit Revivers. Archeologists. We were set on one task - find Pammy. We had to dig through a lot of mess. We were unrelenting. Having taken the journey, I've realized some things.

Gradually and undetectably losing sight of who we were intended to be creates a rupture in our soul. From teenage defiance to mid-life crises, the spirit becomes discontent. For the most part, we humans cannot see this process of self-loss taking place. It's invisible.

As time lapses, the memory bank holds more and more misinformation. For people who grew up with faith, we may blame our religion or creator. We mistrust humanity. We can't repair our brokenness so we bury it. We start to see outside things through the faulty lens through which WE were seen. We become the dysfunction.

In my version of life's story, the traumas piled up like those amazing boulder mountains in Arizona. The traumas were too much. I didn't know it, but I dissociated. Without deciding to or even knowing it happened, I completely unplugged from the feelings I should have been feeling about what was happening. I fragmented into parts.

There was the angry side of me that protected me from aggressive people; that exploded with fury at any sign of potential harm. She was the hyper-vigilant part, always surveying the surroundings to make sure I could anticipate trouble. There was the codependent side that compulsively wanted to help those who couldn't help themselves, even at the expense of my own sanity.

There was the little manager who worked three jobs at once and tried to execute everything perfectly because staying busy kept her from feeling those unbearable feelings. Being perfect gave her some small sense of self-worth. There was the grown-up part that most often stood off to the side. She occasionally stepped in with a word of reason but was overpowered 99 percent of the time by the more emotional parts.

Then, there was the scared part. Just writing it down or saying it out loud used to send a shiver down my arms, through my heart, and into my stomach, where all the shivers came together into one solid, heavy stone that sat uncomfortably in my gut. This is the part that held all the pain and all the memories. This is the dissociated part, hidden way down in the depths of me.

This is my inner child, guarding my spirit from harm; except my spirit doesn't want to live in a box. It wants to be free to co-create with my maker out in the world – to love, to heal, to give, to receive, to learn, to play, and to be. If I was ever going to be free, I needed to talk to my scared part...over and over again. The process is like coaxing her out from under the table. It takes patience and time.

INTO THE
WILDERNESS

One of my favorite recovery books is The Body Keeps the Score – a seminal text by trauma expert Dr. Bessel Van Der Kolk who spent decades in the trenches, working with patients and building new ideas and programs around recovery. Very early in the book's prologue, he illustrates just how expansive our shared suffering is.

"One does not have to be a combat soldier, or visit a refugee camp in Syria or the Congo to encounter trauma. Trauma happens to us, our friends, our families, and our neighbors. Research by the Centers for Disease Control and Prevention has shown that one in five Americans was sexually molested as a child; one in four was beaten by a parent to the point of marks being left on their body; and one in three couples engages in physical violence. A quarter of us grew up with alcoholic

relatives, and one out of eight witnessed their mother being beaten or hit."

If we can agree that suffering – life-changing suffering – is a common experience, we can start to talk about it. What does it mean for all of us? Well, it means as children, when we go through traumatic or disturbing experiences, we have feelings. The feelings can overwhelm our system. When they are not resolved with the help of a safe person in a safe place or when they are repeated over and over, many of us simply go away. Dissociate. To survive, we deny reality. We can become delusional about what is real and what is okay.

It does not take massive amounts of physical violence or molestation, either. It can simply be repetitive emotional manipulation. I know children of narcissists, alcoholics, drug addicts, workaholics and various other extremes, who exhibit some of the same C-PTSD symptoms I have struggled with throughout my life. In fact, I think most people have dissociated *something* and even a small amount of hidden pain blocks our potential to be everything we are intended to be. Billy calls it "unresolved discontent."

We have to smash the idea that painful experiences are like "The Great Secret" of our society. We dance around it. We watch entertaining movies featuring all kinds of traumatizing experiences, but fail to see the true story of our own lives.

Surely, we keep this secret for myriad reasons. We are afraid to face our pain. We are loyal to the dysfunctional structure. We may believe we have mastered it and in our delusion, are better than others; then we cling to some self-righteous position. We appreciate the benefits of dysfunctional relationships over their unhealthiness for us. If we point to the dysfunction that led us astray, we will have to see the dysfunction we created. We will have to face the ways in which we have hurt others.

Or, as Billy always says, "We don't know what we don't know." Sometimes, we just have no idea. So instead, we move on like we're supposed to. Today, I have a healthy defiance against that kind of silence.

I think the reason so many people never fully recover the true and intended part of themselves; never get to experience the kind of absolute wholeness that existed in them briefly the day they were born; never get to wake up every single day grateful and full of purpose – is because going down into your gut to pull that part of yourself out and re-parent him or her to their original state is like venturing out into the wilderness.

You have to get comfortable with the great unknown; to be an explorer. Instead of a compass, a stone, a knife, a pot and a first aid kit – you will need good counsel, people like you to walk with, a great willingness to let go of what you think you know, a strong program and your own belief system.

It requires looking at all the things the scared part has been hiding from, working through them, and slowly releasing them. It also requires releasing the coping mechanisms we created to make up for the dysfunction. There is the pain or trauma, and then there is the subsequent behavior. Often, we toil away at the behavior – the defects, the flaws, the bad character traits – and completely ignore the thing inside that drives them. "Pull yourself up from the bootstraps," we say. "Toughen up."

The ironic thing is, I only have to look at my own story to see, I did that. It did not solve anything. I pulled myself up from the bootstraps. I grew up poor and started working full-time summers baby-sitting at the age of 11. Throughout my late teens and twenties, I worked three jobs at a time. I'd pull shifts that landed me working eighteen hours straight, nap for a few hours, and get back at it.

I finished high school and earned two college degrees. I decided I was out of shape once and instead of just losing a few pounds, I got certified as a personal trainer, earned myself six-pack abs, and built a client base. I acquired an entire suite of gym equipment and opened my own fitness center while working my regular full-time job.

I wrote three books, got them published, and launched my own consulting company on the side. I rose up the executive ladder fast in my industry.

So, was I tough as nails? Yeah. I was, but if you could see my insides, you would paint an entirely different picture of me.

COMPLETE COLLAPSE

The crowd sprawled out before me. An event organizer stood behind the mic. A long introduction rolled off her tongue, citing all my accomplishments. The speech came off flawlessly – an inspirational keynote, my favorite kind of engagement. Audience members made a line beside the podium when it was complete, to ask a question or say thanks. One attendee asked something I often heard and I gave my standard response.

"How do you do it all? You must be so busy. You've achieved so much!"

I laughed and traced my finger in a circle around my temple and said, "I must be a little bit crazy!"

She laughed with me, but she had no clue. When I began the beautiful and grueling journey to resolve the causes of all the chaos inside me, I became stronger than I ever imagined I could be – stronger in a softer way. Stronger and less chaotic. Stronger and less in need of constant activity to distract me from my inner unrest.

It's one thing for a house to be strong against fierce winds because the boards are furiously nailed together. It's another thing for it be strong because someone was wise enough to build a foundation underneath it, and to use nails and glue and steel beams for reinforcement. I was tossed together by a hundred coping mechanisms and the house was falling apart, even though it looked nice and pretty. Could I have held that posture forever – managing all the chaos inside? I don't know, maybe. Some people do. The human mind is resilient, strong, and elastic; but I'm glad I didn't.

I was like a teeter totter that stayed balanced and even – neither side ever touching the ground – by counteracting the weight of my trauma with the coping mechanisms I developed. Of course, every once in a while, one thing outweighed the other and the wood plank came crashing so hard to the ground it splintered. Enough of those and you begin to live in fear all the time.

So, yes, many small crashes led to the final destruction of the machine, but I would say it was something inside – not outside – that led to the final break. Each crack – each splinter – came from the outside.

Marital problems, a crack. Difficulty at work, a crack. Parenting challenges, a crack. And with each external problem, a coping mechanism on the other side of the teeter totter. A drink. Obsessive work. Driving too fast. Fighting.

All along the way, the parts of me hung around the teeter totter at a nearby picnic table. When I wanted to learn how to integrate all these parts into a healthy organism that could function normally in the world, I needed to bring them to one place. My amazing therapist had me conduct an activity.

I would close my eyes and picture them at a picnic table outside – the sun pouring down as they played their parts. They were an unlikely gaggle with seemingly nothing in common, save their commitment to a single goal: hold Pam's shit together. The co-dependent side of me would sit passively on the bench. Little manager was always planning something. The angry part loomed over everyone. My adult side stood back, watching it all. Scared part was nowhere to be seen.

All the while, my spirit – my true self – was locked away and all the parts were there to keep life moving. They had no idea about my spirit but they were vaguely aware of the scared, disheveled child guarding something. They were both terrified of her and ignorant about her role.

When bad things happened in life and the various

PAMELA H. SAY

parts of me did their best to manage, they could always hear her – the scared part – crying, screaming, and calling out for help. They hated it, and they always felt like failures. The guilt and shame were too much to bear. That, combined with a profound sense of loneliness from some unidentifiable space inside, led the parts to act out worse than ever.

I know now that the loneliness growing inside me - bigger and bigger as the years passed by - was my spirit calling out to be released. Unresolved pain is progressive. It grows with time like a tumor. All of it culminated into complete collapse of the tee-ter totter. The weight on each side coupled with a weakness in the wood, caused it to break square in the middle where it crossed over the pipe that held it up.

The wood broke in big chunks that jutted upwards. All the crap on either side spilled everywhere. Talk about rock bottom. I wish I had known I didn't have to wait for that to happen. I could have started healing long before – but I thought I could handle it all. Humans are funny, how we so often have to become desperate before we make a change.

Nevertheless, that was a defining moment. It wasn't an end. It was the most beautiful beginning of my entire life. I was born perfectly me on a summer day in 1976. Then, on a crisp October afternoon in 2016, my spirit was set free. The cage door opened. I was born again - not in the way that we talk about religiously, per se. Rather, my spirit was freed from captivity.

It was everything you'd image being released from a mental prison would be. Delightful. Terrifying. Confusing. Then began the road to recovery and learning how to live again. All the sides of my personality melded into one solid and reasonable human being, even the scared part.

For all those years, she sat outside the cage. She really did not want to keep my spirit there, but she was too paralyzed to do anything. She thought she was weak and powerless. She couldn't help herself, let alone anyone else.

She didn't know that all the while the key to the cage was in her possession; that all the answers were right there in her own mind. It is no surprise. We are so often taught early in life not to trust our own thinking.

She was frozen from action. When anyone wandered too close, the other parts lashed out on her behalf. The adult watched it all, wishing she could do something and knowing it was futile until we could get inside that room, so she gave up. The other parts did their jobs – day in and day out - until that fateful day.

When the machine broke, everyone scattered and the scared part came running outside. Feeling my feelings was beyond anything I can really describe but I learned that feelings won't kill me. Isolation will. I let loose and she talked and talked and talked and talked. I didn't do it alone – I couldn't. She still talks, every single day.

One of my most memorable moments in therapy, at the very end of a particularly painful and difficult EMDR session, my spirit came to my scared part and embraced her. My spirit forgave her for the captivity, praised her for being so strong for so many years, and gave her permission to let go.

It was really in that moment that my spirit became who I truly am and that includes all my defects, which are now beautiful gifts. I am strong but not raging. I am empathetic but not codependent. I am creative but not a compulsive workaholic. I am an adult who isn't scared to speak. I have trauma but it doesn't paralyze me.

So this is me – a woman who, at various times in her life, has experienced and witnessed brutal physical abuse, sexual assault, emotional abuse, manipulation, bullying, and gaslighting to name a few - waking up grateful. Not falling apart in the face of challenge. In the morning, when I rise, I pull the air into my lungs like I did the day I was born. I do it intentionally.

Now you know what I was like, and you know what happened. The pages to follow are my tribute to living grateful every single day. This is the story of my spirit. It is the greatest gift I could ever share. Nothing else really matters. Not money or recognition, jobs, success, or a million friends.

I went in. I found myself again.

PART TWO: THE WINDING ROAD TO GRATITUDE

Write. Learn. Grow. Live. Love. Lead. These are a few of my favorite things – my focus for keeping focused on what matters most. Oh little light, you were so evasive before. I relentlessly sought you and now the room is afire with illumination. You are good for me, little light. Spirit of truth. You are good for everybody. I'll hold tight to my rightful place here.

GIFTED AND ALIVE

*Nobody can write your story but you. It does
not have to be the capturing of a moment in
time. It can be a voice, speaking what will be
into the wind, where it is carried through the
universe until it is true.*

C onsciousness came slow as the residue of a
late night anchored my body in a pile of
a warm blankets. Sleep is utopia when my
spirit is free. That wasn't always the case. As the
mind awoke – quicker than the body – a joy filled the
space where memory lives. Eight hours before, I had
a better kind of New Year's Eve.

It was not the chaotic drunkenness of unbridled
youth. It was not the inevitable bloody mental
battles of doomed relationships; battles perfectly
ignited by a night of loud noises and overstimu-

lation. It was not the pit of despair labeled lone-liness, which I later learned was self-imposed fear and isolation. It was not the terror of dysfunction disguised as loyalty that chained me to people and places where I didn't want to be.

Nope. Just me, Rin and Fin - my daughter and her partner - in my perfectly peaceful little apartment playing board games, watching the ball drop, feasting on pasta, and toasting with a really good bottle of sparkling grape juice. Just enough joy and connection to give the spirit a little leap, dashed with the ideal amount of quietude to put us all at ease.

I can love myself like this, which frees me up to love others - not in a codependent, desperate sort of way. Rather, in a, "I am free, and there's you, and here's me," kind of way.

The sounds from the freeway hummed through my window and so the first day of a new year and a new decade began. A new vision. A deeper understanding. A willingness and a desire to settle into peaceful discovery. What might the decade have in store?

Every single thing life brings, I'm sure. It is no different than before, but I am here – different. I am a woman standing on the mountain top, arms out-stretched; the gruesome journey of unbecoming beneath my feet where all the insight lives, to help me face the day – no, the minute – in front of me.

I commit, each morning, that the day ahead will

be an expression of the best in me. I fall short, but I also succeed frequently. The fallen moments present opportunities to dig deep and uncover the broken pieces – to make something beautiful from them. The successes and the repairs emanate from my greatest gifts.

All humans have gifts.

My child creates masterpieces of amazement with fabric, makeup, wigs, and accessories. What she builds out of her imagination, then puts on her body, walks into the world like a living caricature of genius. She awes me.

My sister Laura captures snapshots of life with her camera, so vividly real and alive the skin on my arm forms tiny bumps. The pictures show a spirit of life I struggle to see in person, with my own eyes. I am grateful for her vision.

Billy pieces together the mechanics of deeply complicated projects though devout study and a picture-perfect memory. His ability to bring massive amounts of confoundingly complex details together to create, is like watching magic.

For me, it is words. Words are the canvas, the paint brush, the pigment, the linseed, the palette, the knife, the room I stand in, the wave of my arm, and the glint in my eye. I love this passion, and in a single moment, I am both genius and never good enough.

We should all wake up free. We should all come to

love our gifts. They are often the very things that give us meaning and joy throughout the process of recovery.

FACING FORWARD

Billy's dad Frank used to say, "One eye on yesterday and one eye on tomorrow makes us cock-eyed today."

The church basement. The parsonage living room. The old school house. The town hall meeting room. The addresses change but the message remains. The faces change but the same spirit dances through the doors.

I pushed the silver bar hard and the fire door swept open, blowing a gust of air into my face. It carried laughter, conversation, and the sound of tables and chairs sliding into place across the tan tile floor. This is me in recovery, facing my history and moving forward into hope.

Dark black coffee percolated in tin-sounding drips.

We waited with paper cups in hand. Three years and three months of recovery. I bet I stood in rooms like these 279 times. I bet there were another 700 phone meetings and gatherings in coffee shops and diners.

Yet, this time felt absolutely alien, new, and uncharted. For three years and three months I had been running through the woods, metaphorically. All the while, I looked backwards. I ran and walked and rested and climbed. As I traversed miles and miles in my mind, my spirit experienced miracles. Yet, always, my eyes were firmly fixed behind me. I believe it was an absolutely necessary part of my process. I needed to connect ALL the dots of the past to the present.

Yet, for some time, it had become boring looking back. Nevertheless, turning forward seemed a strange and confusing task. Whatever lay ahead was completely new; somewhere I'd never been. Looking backward during my emotional journey meant lots of stumbling. I embraced the falls – the unseen roots of massive trees cutting their girth through the earth, straight across the trail. I never saw them coming then, WHAM, a monster wreck of limbs, dirt, spit, hair, blood and dust.

Stumbling hurts, but every emotional wipeout came and went. I got up, kept walking, and - still looking back - saw the root I just tripped over. I had the opportunity to review the root and understand how it got there, where it came from, and why it made me fall. It would all suddenly make sense – the story of my life. Connecting the past to the present was the equivalent of a doctoral education in Pam.

I have this beat-up, bent, written-all-over, yellow workbook that tells a lifetime of stories. Grueling. Punishing. Victorious. There was this one guided exercise where you notice the moments in present-day life that scare you most, then trace them back to a similar feeling in childhood. That exercise was the start of setting me free. Learning what happened, how it shaped me, and how those same feelings today are magnified through unexpressed grief – well, that was mind blowing to me.

So now, here I stand in this recovery room, coffee cup in hand. No one even knows another miracle happened.

Just like that, three years in and my recovery from a lifetime of hurt has taken on a new layer. I have turned my head. I am looking forward now. The roots behind me have their rightful place in the dirt. They are the great dichotomy – beautiful and ugly; powerful and finite – just like me. I appreciate them for offering such depth to my recovery, but now, I am ready. I will travel unhindered. I will look for the horizon in front of me.

My story changes with ease, from dirt and blood and branches, to "the turn." It is a slow-motion picture. My body spins in the sun, eyes bright and hopeful. It is a time to trip less but to remember those roots each time I step over one. Yet, now, I do so without coming undone. It is a state of presence for today. It is another victory won.

WAKING UP GRATEFUL

A Catholic priest prayed over us – hundreds of bikers headed out for a Memorial Day ride. He said, there are potholes in the road. Obstacles on the path. There is difficulty and struggle. You have to get comfortable with the uncomfortable.

Waking. This moment quickly became a critical, magnificent part of my day. To awake with a smile – is this how happy people live? Is this how children who are not traumatized wake up most days; because I am 43 now, and this feels unreal.

Once, no always, waking was dread-laden. It's a common experience I hear people talk about often;

how they are having great fun on Friday night and Saturday. Then, Sunday evening comes and they start to get anxiety. That was me most days. I awoke afraid of the people in my life and the potential failures I would face.

The fear was not conscious. I had no awareness of it. It was like, the light of day peaking the foothills rolled sunbeams down the grassy slope and with it, an ache in my stomach. It rarely went away without aid – a drink, roaring music, adrenaline-inducing activity, extreme exercise, workaholism, dysfunctional chaos. They were all mechanisms to distract me from the discomfort.

Though I kept hope alive and tried to see the beauty in the sunrise, the weight of that ache magnified with time. Unresolved pain gets worse – not better – with time.

A sunrise starts with a cacophony of multi-colored hues and gives way to a vast blue sky. Likewise, my ache went from a concentration of colors in my belly, pulsing with the beating of my heart, to a vast agony that infiltrated all of me. Thoughts crept in. They were bad thoughts, speaking from somewhere outside myself, whispering hopelessness in my ear. So, you'll forgive my absolute, all-encompassing, full-body delight that today is consistently different.

The world awakes, the day breaks, and my own divine Spirit stirs my mind with the most beautiful love song. "Start the day grateful," it sings. As my legs stretch and kick off the veil of night, my spirit dances through me. The ache became serenity. It wasn't easy. There are no easy solutions on this planet – no faster, softer way, as the old-timers say. These things take time, commitment, dedication, practice, and passion.

Three years to this new day. Three years of grief work. Parts work. Step work. Trauma work. Daily morning calls. Two meetings a week. A year and a half of focused therapy. I'm not absent the ache, but it doesn't transform into total loss of self anymore.

It's tough but I believe it is the most important thing we can do for ourselves. People spend thousands of dollars on education and training, and years of effort to become a professional in their field of interest. Some put down thousands and thousands of dollars on a wedding.

Imagine if we added up all the hours we spend sitting in front of a screen over our lifetime. I'm not saying don't do those things, but why is it that giving ourselves a voice and setting ourselves free through the inner journey is so often the last item on our bucket list; the last thing we'll invest in. Are we really that conditioned?

I can't help it. I want more. More than the outside world can give me. I want the best of what's inside me. Sadly, people come and go often from recovery. I see, it's too much for them. Not everyone wants to do this. You have to be like Tiger Woods with golf. You have to want it that bad, because the muscles tire, the spirit cries, and the skin breaks then heals. It is itchy when scar tissue forms. Healing is uncomfortable.

Well, I'm fucking Tiger Woods up in here. Today, I wake up grateful.

PEOPLE NEED PEOPLE

Billy had a date with a woman when we first met. He wasn't sure how it went or what was next. I listened to his story and it became quite clear. "Billy," I said, "You just gotta find your kind of weird." Turns out, a couple years, a divorce, and a lot of recovery later, that weirdo was me. We should all find our weird.

My People. I love you. Some people stay right there by your side all along the way. It's amazing.

I once birthed a human being. I fought for fourteen hours to see her gasp that first breath into her tiny little lungs. I fell so deeply in love. She is absolute beauty to me and I see who God intended her to be.

She has Autism and ADHD, some depression, and anxiety. She is also pure strength, unbridled creativity, love, loyalty, deep thinking, and flashes of next-level maturity. Yeah, it is hard sometimes, but it is also so very easy. What a joy to stand by her side.

There are people who have been that unconditional to me. For example, my mom, Laura and Billy look at me and see exactly who I am – when I'm broken, when I'm healing, and even when I'm feeling a little crazy. They don't see me through their own lens, nor do they only see what's wrong with me.

Even more importantly, they step out from the veil and show me who they are – truly are. That's a feeling of love that is hard to measure for the recipient.

Billy is often other-worldly. He has done a lot of the work necessary to "know thyself." Our conversations take on a different level.

We missed our normal Saturday morning ritual of breakfast and a meeting. He was tired from surgery. The work week left me needy for a day of coffee, Netflix and munchies. I was surprised when our early morning call log said three hours when it felt like fifteen minutes, but that's me and Billy. I get him and he gets me. The depth of that relationship is a direct gift of recovery.

I have other people too. When COVID-19 forced us all inside many people recovering from a wide variety of addictions and emotional ailments struggled. People need people who have walked in their shoes when they are facing their biggest inner battles. If doing it alone was the solution we'd all just hide out for a few weeks and be healed. I found myself struggling when the regular things I relied on for strength went away.

After two weeks of isolation in my small upstairs apartment, staring into a computer or a phone screen at videos of faces, my psyche started wavering. I called a very small handful of my closest friends in recovery. We followed all the government guidelines. There were only six of us. We sat six feet apart outside. Everyone brought their own chairs so no one touched anything.

The cold air that danced across the surface of icy Lake Erie, traversed Route 5 and Route 90, and made its way through the buildings of my apartment complex. It blew thirty-some-degree shivers through my body. I snuggled into my winter coat and fluffy hat, sat right there in the grass, and had one hell of a meeting.

RECOVERY IS CATCHY

> *"You know it's like, I dunno you... you float out... float out at sea then one day you find a port say, 'I'm gonna stay here a few days.' Few days 'comes a few years. Then you forgot where you're going in the first place. Then you realize you don't really give a shit about where you was goin', cause you like where you at."* Noodles, A Star is Born

Presents littered the living room floor in piles around the tree. Our little apartment got messy, but I wasn't worried. It was so small, it took no time at all to clean.

The home I sold after the divorce took a long time to clean. Back then, the work week left me exhausted. Nights and weekends demanded all the other things. Home cooked meals. Clothes spinning in the laundry. Wheels on the cart clicking as it bore the weight of groceries. Mediating endless battles between my partner and my offspring. Then ensuring some facet of my child's life was filled with joy and discovery.

She and I did everything. We screamed as we plummeted two hundred feet on our favorite roller coaster. I laid in the grass watching her as she practiced cheerleading or soccer. I stood in hallways while she attended dance and gymnastics classes. I watched her in wonder in plays.

Later, we went to endless conventions for costuming. We took trips to the mall, music booming in the car while we sang and danced and giggled. Sometimes we took those same trips and they were tear-filled, as she poured out the pain of people not understanding. We took turns walking weirdly and laughing. We made funny faces while doing our makeup. A million times, I picked up and dropped off her friends. I would do just about anything to give her a smile in the blowing winds.

Now, don't get it twisted. I was NOT the picture of perfection. Other memories intertwine.

My marriage was broken. I pleaded for fixing in desperate down-on-your-knees-kind-of-pleas for years. She witnessed all of that. A human cannot carry on in desperation and maintain their sanity.

At times, he enraged me. I could get ugly. Sometimes I would tear out of the driveway with my foot pressed on the gas pedal and hit the highway. I would try to calm down while the world blew past me.

There were times I threw something or punched the wall so hard my knuckles turned purple and knotty. I ran crying and screaming. Other times, I just shut down completely. I went blank. I stopped feeling. I also took to drinking. I tried to do it gently – late at night after my daughter went to bed; but there were occasions she saw me that way and she made it very clear. She did not like it. Worst of all, I reacted out of PTSD to normal little things. I think that scared her the most.

She was diagnosed with ADHD but it didn't explain all the other things happening with her – lack of eye contact, blunt interrupting, talking and not listening, and socially inappropriate comments people wrongly labeled as defiant. She couldn't count change at 16, couldn't ride a bike, would shower for an hour and forget to use soap, and expressed herself primarily through clothing. I could write a novel on the sounds that scared her to screaming, the fear of people who weren't me, and the melt downs and sleeping.

She would plead with me about her intentions and I believed her. No one else but my mom seemed to agree at that time. Teachers, coaches, family, friends, counselors – all labeled her with words, looks, and whispers to others in secrecy. Their eyes declared flawed, defective, wrong, untrustworthy.

I remember one experience where this couple that had just met us joined together with my partner at the time. Together, they asserted judgements on her. It is incredible the lengths people will go to control others, or to prove they are right – regardless of how it destroys the spirit of another human being. Fortunately, I'm not a momma bear. I'm a momma beast. I took the brunt of their accusations and did my best to protect her from it.

That does not mean I am unrealistic. I've come to understand I harm her if I practice codependency. However, it DOES mean I will stand between her and anyone who would tear her spirit down, until she learns how to stand in that place for herself. I'll teach her. I'll insist.

Someone should have done that for all of us. Recovery is allowing your inner child back out and allowing your adult self to protect him or her – to stand in the gap and allow that child inside to finally grow up.

Throughout those years, I worked the system the best I could. I used all the parts of me to pave the way for her safety; but it wasn't enough. I couldn't save her at that time from society, and she was bottoming. Things got pretty scary for a while. I relied heavily on her therapist for support.

So help me God if I didn't get a little testy with the world when she got diagnosed with Autism at the age of 17. One particular person responded to the news in one sentence: "So... what... is she going on disability now?" Later, he suggested to her that she not tell anyone, which was the same comment he made years before when she told him she was gay. "It's nobody's business," he would say. I translate that to mean, "It makes me uncomfortable so don't live your truth. Hide who you really are."

This was one of the people who so brutally judged her and took everything she did personally. He offered no apology or even a willingness to talk about what the new information would mean or how the past may have been affected by not knowing. I share this not to demean anyone, nor out of unresolved bitterness. I share it because I believe it is much more common than we think. It may be one of the most common human experiences – subtle shaming or the simple refusal to communicate. Both drive the spirit inward.

As a mom in search of my own healing, I learned how to replace bitterness and unbridled anger with deliberate focus. I became crystal clear. Sitting here today in this smaller, safer place – in our tiny little apartment - a mess of Christmas bliss sprawled out before me, she and I are free.

She sleeps in her room quietly. Seventeen years old and we're walking now – briskly. We aren't running and falling and bleeding. We aren't standing frozen. We have a path with sign posts. We have each other and, hand intertwined with hand, we step out of the trees into our destiny.

She cries and questions, but she is also aware of everything. This messy little place that takes me fifteen minutes to clean is nirvana. It's a reflection of my recovery and her recovery, because recovery is catchy.

NEVER
SURRENDER

Yesterday, patches of thick wet snow slid off the side of the airplane, doused in de-icing spray as it idled near the runway.

Buffalo, New York.

Today, the dark morning covers the crisp cool air like a blanket. Sixty-some degrees at 6:33 a.m.

Gilbert, Arizona.

"Wake up grateful," my mind reminds me. Cars hum on a nearby highway. Big, bold stucco homes sit close together in lines and circles around cul-de-sacs. Denise's patio feels like a perfect gathering place for friends and family.

The patio television played the Buffalo Bills game intermittently for smokers last night, when they stepped out from the living room to light up. There are three seating areas out back, a fire pit, and a fenced in pool with star lights hanging from the top rail. She makes it feel like home even for distant travelers. That's a gift.

Lots of personalities packed the house last night – nearly everyone replanted from somewhere in Western New York. They donned Bills' jerseys and bellowed excitedly or angrily at the tv screen. The game was tied into overtime, but the Bills lost and unfortunately, it knocked them out of the playoffs. Honestly, it was one of the few time in my life that, as an adult, I really sat and attentively watched a football game. It was interesting, but more than anything, I liked watching the fans.

Bills' fans are rugged and passionate, but out of all adjectives, they are absolutely sedulous. Unrelenting. They never surrender. They never back down. They're Bills' fans, Bills' fans, Bills' fans – when the sun comes up and when the sun goes down.

I love that kind of toughness. Western New Yorkers are a rugged lot. I'm proud to be one. When Mattie Ross approached Marshall Rueben "Rooster" Cogburn and said, "They tell me you're a man with true grit," I'm not certain she even knew what she was talking about. By the end of the movie, she knew.

Grit doesn't develop from a little toughness or pumping irons in the gym. It doesn't come from a single instance of peacocking in the face of a challenge. It comes from suffering. The Buffalo Bills have faced so many challenges as a team and a fan base, but they never lose hope. They never stop fighting with the same energy. On any given game day you can find the Bill's Mafia painted up like a group of red, white and blue Gene Simmons, tailgating in a blizzard outside the stadium. That's how I feel about my life's journey. Nothing is going to stop me.

UNLEARNING

"I had no idea what the future was like but I knew I didn't want to wear shoes." Flea, Acid for the Children

The day's agenda was breakfast then golf at 11:15 – me, Billy, Mike and Denise. Thank you, God and recovery, for helping me to learn how to have fun and play when my old tendency was to isolate and be afraid.

An outing like this used to bring all sorts of anxiety. I'd wake up scared, worry about what to wear, and get angry if I didn't have perfect hair. The whole time I was with people, I would have this sense of myself, like I was aware of every feeling in my body and I could hear every word I said.

Meanwhile, another voice was criticizing it all as it

came out. Then part of me would watch everyone and look for cues. Are they disappointed? Are they judging me? If I thought that were true, I'd overcompensate the other way.

Another thing inside was gruelingly working to control my emotions so nothing showed. I could carry on with a smile without anyone realizing all this was happening. Sometimes, if it came to be too much, everything inside would just shut down. All that remained was the smile on my face.

Have you ever looked deep enough to notice when someone's smile is on the surface and not of the spirit? I won't call it fake – just the best they can surmise. It hides just beneath the eyes. I notice it more now – and I crave to know their kid inside.

This day is different! I popped up out of bed excited. I have to admit, golf can be one of my favorite ways to play when it's not driving me crazy. It sits in the top three with motorcycle riding and writing. I put on my outfit and hat and bounded downstairs.

The crisp morning woke me right up. Billy, Mike, Denise and I made our way to a great farm-to-table restaurant nearby. We ate a hearty breakfast, talked a lot, and looked at a super cool tree out back. It bore a sign that said, "Don't climb. Risk of scorpion bites." I saw orange and lemon trees for the first time in my life, we golfed and I had some great shots, then we tiredly returned to the house, satisfied.

Very little of the old crap crept up and to a much lesser degree. It's not that it never happens. I still struggle with my issues but the turnaround time is getting shorter and shorter.

Sometimes I notice things and wonder what someone is thinking, but I try not to obsess. I give people room to speak up if they need to. I state a boundary, though sometimes still a bit too emotionally. I don't over apologize anymore. If I do something wrong, I just make amends and move on.

Things are simpler now. They are not perfect; they are a work in progress, and the progress is made by maintaining the foundation I have laid. I rely on good counsel, support, meetings, and prayer. More importantly than anything, I allow my true self to have her voice.

Back at the house after a delightful day of golf, I laid down on the bed. The daily reflection popped onto my phone screen in all its spiritual glory, like it was written for me and only me.

It was not. Time has shown me, I'm not unique. Most people share many of the same qualities and that is comforting. Even when the reflection or affirmation seems written just for me, I know these are universal truths. When we think we are the only one going through something, we give ourselves an excuse to isolate which only serves to keep us sick.

The reflection essentially said that, for many of us,

there is a moment when we find ourselves trapped in a dilemma that has been growing inside for years – and that we are standing at a crossroads. We do not want to continue but we do not want to let go. As such, we will come to know deep and profound inner pain. If we stand there indecisively forever, the pain will remain. It said, we may wish for the end, but this defining moment can be the start of something new.

There was a time I wished for one kind of an end. I thought an end of my life would be an end of my suffering. Though I would never do it, just the fact that the thought lived in my head tortured me. Then, someone told me my suffering could end another way - through recovery and support. So, I wished for a new kind of end – the end of my conditioning. The beginning of unlearning. I chose recovery.

THE GREAT
HUMAN CHARTER

I stand perfectly still as the earth turns, the sun rises in the east, the clouds move, and my heart beats.

I have to confess something. This book is a vessel I'd like to send out into the world – yes – but I started it very much for me. I saw this great unattributed meme on New Year's Eve. I know that's not very cultured, but whatever.

It said, "Today is the first blank page of a 365-page book. Write a good one." I was just emerging into my new state of being, looking forward and living with gratitude. It wasn't a passing thing. It was consistent and comforting.

I am 43 at the time of this writing, and I started journaling when I was around eight years old. For 35 years, I had been writing down all the bad things. The idea of composing a book of celebration that connects the dots of the past to the present, reveals the miracles of my life, celebrates the joy of everyday, and tackles challenges – that sounded GREAT To me!

This exercise is meant to be a state of my developing; the practice of capturing snapshots of what is around me; being present and seeing; saying "thank you" to the creator of all things, who is out in the heavens and simultaneously, inside me. It is the ups and downs and in-betweens.

Ralph Waldo Emerson said, "Write in your heart that every day is the best day in the year," and Walt Whitman said, "Happiness, not in another place but this place...not for another hour, but this hour."

So, all we have to see is the hour we are in? In doing so, we can accept suffering as a human experience? We no longer have to anticipate it, fight it, or regret it? THen what? We feel what we need to feel about it, and let it go? We understand that we all have it and we need not compare it?

Who is to say whether one human's experience with suffering is any easier or worse than another. It is, in many ways, the great human charter. Letting someone into our suffering is the ultimate act of vulnerability, and contains the potential to build unbreakable bonds. Sometimes we demand that others take responsibility for our suffering or do something to end it. I think only we can end the suffering in our own minds - but we do it through connections with others who have walked in our shoes.

The little airplane tattooed on my left forearm memorializes Richard Wayne's Say's love for the craft. My father drew model airplane plans and sold them around the world from the old wooden table he built in our dining room. A cigarette hung between his lips as he created mechanical masterpieces that actually flew.

It was his art – the reflection of all his greatest gifts. He was featured in magazines and I remember this guy from Ireland or some distant place flying out to meet him. He never made any money off it. He should have. He was so brilliant.

My dad learned drafting while in reform school and later, prison. He was just a boy from a broken home. He stole a car and they sent him away. My dad was amazing. Despite our shared suffering, my father's intensity, love for history, engineering ability on only a GED, and childlike delight when a plane he made of balsa, glue and mylar buzzed its way into the wild blue – moved me.

The day he died the grief overwhelmed my spirit. Human suffering. So, Emerson, how was that the best day of my life? Whitman, how could I find happiness in that hour?

Maybe in that moment I could not see it, but I see it now. He held me as a child. He cradled me in his arms when I cried. He also hurt me deeply with his own PTSD. He worked his hours away driving 400 miles a day to provide for me. And when the last breath slipped from his lips – his head hanging restfully – I was there. I held his hand in the living room where we danced the jitterbug, sat quietly listening to Johnny Cash and Little Richie, and where he made me learn all that WWII history.

It was the end of his suffering. He never got to find out all these things. He never got this depth of recovery, but I did get to see his little kid inside more than once. I picture that little kid now, dancing and smiling. Grief is just all my love for him pounding in my heart like an orchestra playing our favorite symphony – Carmina Burana – just for him and me. I loved him deeply.

Then, there is another kind of suffering – the kind that landed me in trauma therapy. For some of us, there are big horrors. So, what of that Whitman? Any answers Emerson?

Even those experiences planted seeds of resilience and a healthy ferocity in me. I can channel that into good things, and it's not only me.

I met an African woman once who was an adult

student at the college where I worked. She was taking nursing. She came to a donor reception to tell her story. She walked in wearing all white, as were each of her five children. They were a masterpiece! I knew her. We had interacted occasionally, but when she stood behind the podium I felt the presence of a spiritual queen.

She told her story of civil war. People were gunned down in her village. She escaped to a far-away place – a beach. She could speak English so the American embassy hired her to help the other refugees. She spent years working, re-settling, and living in camps. Finally, the U.S. gave her and her children asylum. She came to Western New York in winter and one of the first things they had to do was acquire winter coats. This was certainly a new world, far from everything she knew.

She was a single mom starting over from nothing. She opened a business, got a degree, and became a nurse. She dreamed of going back to help rebuild her country. The horrors of war cannot always be shared in polite conversation. We only heard a piece of what she endured. Still, she smiled effortlessly. She talked about blessings. Her kids reflected the same spirit of release. She did the therapy and I'm sure it wasn't easy, but here she was, a woman on a mountain top with all the insight beneath her feet. Happiness was written in her heart.

The hour I was harmed is certainly not and never

will be the happiest hour of my life. However, if I overcome it, the hour suddenly takes on much more meaning. I become all I am meant to be.

FINDING MY
TRUTH

The motorcycle carried us effortlessly up the road that cut through a mountain of rigid, jagged stone. Prickly bushes dotted the rocks, interrupted sporadically by tall, round cacti in light green. We drove in and out of vastly different landscapes through the course of the day. We saw white stone cut in sheets for salt mining, red boulders pointing toward the sky in straight lines, the brightest blue lake I'd ever seen, snow atop a mountain, and a forest of green.

A day can be so beautiful it feels like a dream.

Later that night, something happened that triggered my PTSD. After that, I floated through a few days. I wrote nothing. The traumatic stress swept over me. At the moment it happened, I felt the adrenaline flood my bloodstream. I reacted quickly and angrily.

Back in the old days, flashbacks would overtake me. I remember a particularly bad episode. I was laying in bed when suddenly, I thought I smelled something that reminded me of one of my abusers. There was no smell at all, apparently. It was all in my mind.

Earlier in the day something happened very subtly and the fear was already settling in by the time I laid down for bed. As I lay there and the thoughts scrambled through my head, I reverted to a living memory. The smell was as real to me as if it was there. I leaped from the sheets and started looking out the windows.

"He's here," I kept shouting. "He's come to kill me." I was circling the house frantically when it occurred to me, my daughter is in her bedroom. What if he climbs in the window? I woke her up abruptly and locked us in the spare bedroom while I convinced someone else to grab a weapon and walk the property. A single episode like that could lead to weeks of exhaustion and confusion.

Today, with the help of significant therapy, I see it all happening. The reactions are much less scary. My therapist once told me, "If you notice the anxiety at the very beginning, earlier in the day, you can tend to yourself before you careen into that kind of instability."

She was right. When I feel the changes in my heart

beat, I have an opportunity to quickly take care of my needs. I self-sooth and if I have to, I leave the situation. But even when I just get snippy, I can feel profoundly guilty. Now, I know not to blame anyone else or even myself.

So, when this minor trigger hit me after our beautiful day on the motorcycle, I lost a couple days to "drifty" thinking. I participated in the last day of golf, the trip back to Buffalo, and a day of rest and recovery. I was edgy and sensitive. My mind wandered to the meaning of things.

Quite often in the aftermath of a trigger, I turn into "Dr. Pam the Philosopher." The day was 1-11. I decided to let my superstitious side come out to play. I saw the numbers a few times and I wondered, what do the scribes say? What do repeated ones mean? The web site began by explaining that the law of attraction will pull people and situations into your life that match your energetic vibration. You create your own physical reality and you don't even need words or actions – just feelings.

Good God. That's a great description of so many things in life. How many times in my life have I felt something so deeply, acted on those feelings, and caused results that matched them? I remember reading the Art of Happiness by the Dalai Lama and he said something like, when you act on your fear, you cause that fear to become reality.

So often we really do think ourselves into our experiences. Once I see that, I can become a CON-SCIOUS CREATOR. For some of us, that requires undertaking a long and deliberate process to repro-gram our thought patterns.

The scribes continued, put the past behind you and move forward with confidence. "The feeling of dis-tress is a recycling of a past event that has not been released energetically."

It took a long time to assess the past and see how it affected my present, but the affirmation came at a perfect time – the time when I was ready to move forward. People often surmise there is no solution to PTSD or even to a painful past full of secrecy. There is. I'm living it.

After all my writings about turning forward and embracing the day, this was the final, bolded state-ment on Willow Soul: "Always remember, you'll know you are headed in the right direction when you no longer have an interest in looking back."

Thank you, God. Thank you, universe. Thank you, recovery. Thank you for whispering these truths to me and encouraging me, "Keep going, girl. Keep going. You are operating from a place of truth."

After several days post-trigger, I let myself rest so I could awake with a new mindset.

COURAGE TO CHANGE

Three of us sat in the small parsonage turned office building. The old living room was packed full of forty-year-old couches, chairs, lamps and tables. Most of the lamps didn't work. The chairs squeaked loudly every time you shifted your body weight. Cars buzzed by outside the big picture window.

The meeting was over. It was powerful. We all felt it and we all knew we all felt it. Billy wore a soft smile. I could see he was delighted. He loves truth.

The other member looked slightly stunned but in a good way – like when you have been changed right there in a moment's time but you don't fully realize it yet. It dawns on you slowly over the days to come but there, in that moment, it's like the impact point. Slow. Confusing. Exciting.

I don't know what the heck I looked like, but I felt absolutely abuzz inside. Even more, I felt love and appreciation for my fellows. Walking alongside others who want truth as bad as you do and are willing to go deep inside to get it – no matter how scary or temporarily disruptive it is – is a gift beyond gifts.

Sitting there, looking at the two of them after all three of us dug deep, exposed our pain, fought forward, found truth, and claimed it – well, how could we not feel a sense of family? I didn't just wake up grateful that day, I went to bed grateful too.

We talked about powerlessness and unmanageability. I was always powerless over other people's dysfunction, but when you are trapped in it, you do everything you can to try and control the outcome, control the environment, and prevent and minimize the pain.

I held my breath, clenched my teeth, and tensed my body. I watched for signs, manipulated situations, and people pleased. I practiced perfectionism, shut down, ran, and worked to escape. They were all ways to try and have some power over someone else's sickness, addiction, dissociation or rage.

I survived but my life became unmanageable. No one can hold that much tension inside forever. I remember as a little girl all the way to my rock bottom at the age of 40, falling asleep in a curled-up ball, all my muscles contracted, holding myself in – even holding my breath.

It was strange in recovery to notice that. Eventually, I started to fall asleep sprawled out and relaxed, like babies do when they're safe. It was different than how I slept my entire life. It felt strange. Sometimes I still fight the urge to ball myself up and squeeze myself in.

It took seven full months in recovery before I realized I was powerless to change anyone, and that carrying my childhood coping mechanisms into adulthood was longer necessary. I could let go and focus on what I could change – myself. That was a defining moment.

IMPOSTER IN
MY SHOES

A new day brings new dreams. I often dreamt of the pinnacle of achievement – President of the University. I saw them at graduation ceremonies in their large, velvet robes with puffy sleeves and stripes across the arms, their pentagon shaped caps, and medals dangling down their chests. They looked like wizards.

They held a revered place, respected by most as they spoke from the podium with ease and command. I worked my way up from entry level to my first Vice Presidency before forty, then my second. I got my MBA and was accepted into a doctoral program. I had a mentor and was told colleges would be knocking down my door with opportunities. I was good at my job. It's where I thought I always wanted to be.

Then this nagging feeling set in later in recovery. It

was telling me to slow down, take it easy, enjoy life. That feeling used to creep into my chest once in a blue moon but now it was full-fledged consuming me. In the past, I would crush it with workaholism.

What a stupid thought, I'd think. Also, who am I without all my achievements? That poor little girl? That abused young lady? The one surrounded by a crowd in a fist-fight outside of middle school? Am I the daughter of.... mother of.... sister of.... Am I nobody? I'd get angry and think, NO! I'm an author, a VP, and a future President. THAT'S me.

So actually, as it turns out, I'm none of those things. The joke's on me.

They may be my experiences, but they aren't ME. I am simply me. This spirit in this temporary body is me. When I'm tapped into it fully, I stop acting as any of those other things. I become an expression of joy, gratitude, love and serenity.

I have a voice to use to set boundaries. I get to say yes or no to anything. I suffer physically and emotionally, but my spirit lives through every suffering. Like a kid in a park or playing ball or making art – I am the source of all creativity.

I have no idea what I'll do now. If I finish my doctorate, I'll do it gently. If I get a presidency, it will be with some boundaries. If the artwork of my life becomes something completely different, so be it. I'm open to whatever is revealed in this painting.

Once I decided to let go, just like that, the universe affirmed me. The affirmation the day I wrote this said do not live life as a fraud; as your false self. Find out who you really are. Cut the chains between who you really are and this imposter that walks in your shoes. If you do, you'll experience the greatest sort of freedom.

HIGHER PURPOSE

"Mama, well she told me, time is such a wonderful gift. You're not running out. You're really running in." Trevor Hall, You Can't Rush Your Healing

A lot happened yesterday. Together with my Middle States Standard II Team, I performed the song, "Let's Get Ethical" from The Office at College Assembly in front of 300 people. I presented an update on funding for a major capital project and pitched the naming opportunities. I gave an inspirational speech positioning us as the "University of the Future," including showing my video-taped interview with Mayor Jenn Daniels from Gilbert, Arizona.

I attended the Buffalo Niagara Partnership Advocacy Agenda Rollout. I finalized three Board presentations, drafted a reorganization proposal, studied fundraising and alumni participation numbers, and ideated some staffing opportunities.

You know what stirred my soul yesterday? The thirty-minute car ride home playing John Frusciante's Before the Beginning instrumental from the Empyrean album on repeat.

The sounds in his music bring to mind outer space or the depths of the ocean. He transports me to the throne of God. It's like being devoid of physicality in the great expanse of being. The chords echo in my spirit and I know John co-created this with the same spirit that co-creates with me when I'm tapped into infinity.

True creation, or better said, pure creation derived from the source of all truth, is what I care most about these days.

It is so many things. When I bring that spirit of truth and creativity into my profession as a non-profit fundraiser, people are moved to tears or action. When I lead with authenticity, people are willing to work harder than I ever dreamed. When I let go and tap into truth when I'm speaking, the audience members say things like, "that was life changing!"

I understand all of that because I'm a human being who, when I feel, see and hear truth, I want follow.

Truth is that beautiful, altruistic goal and higher

purpose of a thing. It is getting to who someone is, not what their experience conditioned them to be. It is untainted like the newborn child, the boundless puppy, the field of daisies, and the full green tree. It is the quiet morning sky. It is you and I.

Listing to John in my car, the tears streamed down my cheeks.

Later, tired from the day, I fell fast asleep.

LETTING GO

Sometimes shit goes down. People get crazy. The texts blew up my phone as an acquaintance let off a fury of emotional rounds, akin to that of an automatic assault rifle, from a desperate mental state.

I pictured him red-faced; his eyes and brow curled up with rage. I understand venting. This was poison. Daggers. A heavy lead pipe. Anything to beat the life out of the anguish in his heart – which he inevitably was pinning on someone or something else.

It had nothing to do with me, but somehow, in his mind, I was the bounty hunter. I was supposed to hunt down a solution, hold it hostage, and present it to him so he could lash out a punishment. This is what I like to call alcoholic insanity. Once upon a time I would run around and do all his bidding. There was also a time I was somewhat like him.

I responded with a few texts, kept my cool, and

stayed focused. I didn't let him disrupt my emotional sobriety. My daughter sat on the other end of our blue couch expressively relating new discoveries. All the while, a relentless barrage of notifications lit up my phone, the sound of each one interrupting our flow. I turned the volume down.

Listening to my daughter, the phone screen illuminated with each new text. My heart beat quickened with anxiety. I turned the phone upside down. Later, when I was alone, I read the words on my screen. The texts were littered with accusations, character assassinations, threats and posturing. I did what I do. I stopped texting. I went to a meeting. I talked about what happened. I listened to people with more experience than me.

Back home, I prayed about it. I said what I needed to say to him, clearly, and without all the drippy co-dependent sympathy I would have had before recovery. I went to bed tired and woke up tired. I had a hangover and I wasn't even the one drinking. I asked God for some more help, journaled about it, talked to a trusted friend, and suddenly, just like that, there it was. The clouds opened up.

The blue sky peeked out through the hole, which was growing and expanding as the sun burned away the haze. The wind carried off the speckled clouds that remained. Standing out on my front porch in the wee early glory of the morning, this issue resolved itself internally. It took less than 15 hours.

I closed my eyes. The cold air bit at me, but the warm sun was on my cheeks.

I do not try to save people anymore. They have to make that choice for themselves. To the ones that do – I'll walk with you.

LEARNING TO
LOVE MYSELF

One of my old journals sat in a pile of little books on the nightstand. Journals are like my paint brushes. Instead of stems speckled with old paint sticking out of a cup, I have books of all shapes and sizes sprawled out on surfaces throughout the house.

Created by the company Orange Circle, this journal was categorized as a "deconstructed" piece – a fitting name. I bought that journal immediately before my bottom. It marked the start of my unbecoming.

There was a name for the journal printed just above the UPC code. Solitude Tree. The journal's exposed binding, rough canvas cover, and weathered edges made it the perfect companion. From first entry to last it spanned two years, two months and sixteen days. I usually plow through a few journals a year.

The first few entries, printed with perfect precision, reminded me of the most organized kitchen cupboards I had ever seen. The food cupboards were full of little plastic tubs labeled, stacked, and faced in perfect alignment. No dish or cup or cooking utensil was out of place. Not a speck of dust lay waste – inside or outside those cupboard doors. My journal had to be perfect. It just had to be.

Inside the pages, I could see my parts at play. Little manager was in work mode back then and she cut like a knife with the pen. I was going to write a book on "A Year of Love." I had this idea that the only thing that really mattered in life was Jesus' Greatest Commandment to love God with all your heart, soul and mind and love your neighbor as yourself; but that most of us failed at execution.

I burned with frustration when I saw religious elitism that made me feel judged instead of loved; but was equally as sad when families professed Christ's way but destroyed their children with dysfunction.

I wondered why some Christians talked so much about rules, instead of training their congregations day after day on the deepest meaning of love, how to live it in an actionable way, and how to differentiate between love and manipulation. Little did I know, I myself had such a long way to go.

Nevertheless, in that moment, I was moved by the Jesus I knew. I read the Bible front to back and I saw a guy with dirty shoes who fought the institution and hung out with fringe dwellers; who stood up against any form of wielded power, even when single individuals made harsh judgements. I learned so much from him. So, I planned to study love for a year, find out what it means to me and others, and capture the spirit of the commandment as a testimonial to real healing in the world.

I actually wrote this on day one: "Love is learning oneself well enough to feed the soul so that it is full, positive and thriving; so you can be a mirror of love for others." Even though I wrote it, I couldn't possibly comprehend the depth of what that meant. Where the hell did that come from inside me? It was one of those moments. I had no idea what I was talking about, but it foreshadowed something to come. Maybe my spirit was speaking that truth into the universe, from inside her cage – waiting, knowing, there was a way.

I struggled kicking the book off. I remember praying about it. "God, help me see the truth in this process." The first entry was in January, the next in May, then September. I remember what was happening in the gaps. My husband and I were bottoming. An important friend was relapsing. My beautiful child was grappling with severe depression. My dad was dying, and I was trying to hold everything together.

I often found myself deep in the woods. Spring, summer, fall winter – it didn't matter. It could be a blizzard. I'd walk and walk and walk until I was exhausted. I would ache inside, then come home and drink and write.

My spirit was calling for release; screaming from inside for freedom. I was beginning to hear it and that was terrifying. My natural inclination was to run. I always had a hair-trigger fight or flight reflex. Fight occurred more frequently but when flight kicked in, I was like Speedy Gonzalez or Superman flying so fast he made the earth turn.

One time, my Aunt Jeanne was down visiting and we were all sitting around the table talking and eating. My dad said something and like kids often do, I made a face when I disagreed. It was not overtly disrespectful. I simply disagreed expressively, but in under two seconds, he rose up from his chair, leaned his torso forward across the table, and slapped my face so hard my body launched sideways. Down, hard, on the floor I landed.

Shame and humiliation burned in my cheeks and like a tight spring, I bounced fast off the floor and sprinted out the back door. I remember catching a glimpse of my Aunt Jeanne's face as I quick-checked to see if he was behind me. It was distorted with horror.

He tried to catch me and I nearly laughed when he slipped in the grass and the gap between us grew. I ran for probably twenty blocks full speed. I got to the convenience store uptown and found a bunch

PAMELA H. SAY

of my friends. We started walking like nothing ever happened.

Now all these years later, my body wanted to run. I obliged. I packed my bags, hopped on a plane, and left. In October 2018, I published an article in Advancing Philanthropy magazine where I recounted the story:

> "In an attempt to get away, I flew my daughter and I to Taos, New Mexico, on the opposite side of the country. To say the trip felt like my own painful pilgrimage would be an understatement. I visited a place called El Sanctuario de Chimayo, a little compound in the New Mexico mountains dating back to the 1800's. Soldiers and sailors subjected to the Bataan Death March made it an annual pilgrimage to give thanks for their deliverance from the war and to memorialize their suffering after returning home.
>
> The sanctuary was brilliant. Adobe walls. Rounded archways. Outdoor worship areas. Trees and fences covered by hundreds of rosaries. A stark silence. Serenity. I made my way to the inner chamber of the healing room. A perfectly round hole in the ground contained dirt said to be blessed. I picked it up, closed my eyes, and cried out a prayer for deliverance. When I walked away I hoped to leave my pain on the dirt floor. Not much happened in that moment,

and frankly, I missed home. I knew I couldn't run from my mind anymore, but what I did not know was that something would be waiting for me – a profound rock bottom and hope for a new beginning."

Back in my journal, about a year passed from the time I said love was a mirror and prayed for God to show me the truth. I was supposed to be wrapping up my book, which I decided I would call "The Love Doctrine." I had ten pages written when I walked away from it and instead, walked into the rooms of recovery.

Funny, looking back, I see I never walked away from it at all. I was always learning to love myself, it just took an unexpected route. So, where I thought I'd write this intellectual, spiritual masterpiece based on the brilliance of my abilities, I wrote this in my journal instead:

"I was going to study love from every aspect, talk to others, and ultimately hoped to bring practical meaning to the philosophical overture Christ professed as 'the greatest of these.' I didn't even get started before life ran over me like a semi-truck annihilates a piece of fruit that fell from a tree and tumbled into the road.

I was the fruit. The truck was a trigger. My insides exploded into pulp on the hot pavement – too destroyed to ever regain who I was before that; the only option left, to figure out how to be something new. Be juice. Be applesauce. Be jam. But never again could I be that shiny piece of fruit hanging by a stem from the tree by the side of the road."

I was in pain. I thought I was destroyed; not realizing I was still there, just waiting. I had to clear away the debris to see that. Some people would get resentful with God, angry at the world, and self-loathing for the difficulties that arose. I don't know. I just had hope. Even as a kid in the midst of pain and confusion, I always believed and what I understood to be God always – always – delivered me.

The 180 pages that followed in my journal were a detailed account of my first year and five months in recovery. The epiphanies showed up like the grand finale at the fireworks display, page after page. I guess, sometimes, prayers get answered in really unexpected ways.

I learned to love myself by learning to know myself. How can you really love something you cannot understand? It's like saying, "I LOVE snow," when you have lived on a tropical island your entire life. You might love the look of snow. You might even feel an affinity for it, but will you love it after fifteen years of shoveling, after being stranded in traffic during rush hour on Route 90, after slipping and falling? Today I can honestly say I know me, all the parts of me.

FINDING
ASSOCIATIONS

The snow came down wet and turned instantly to water on the windshield, overworking the wipers. Cars backed up on Route 5 forming a line of red tail lights under a grey sky. It was our regular morning call on my commute to work. Billy and I dreamed of getting away. He put an offer in on a second home in Arizona and the process began, preparing for the change.

He was in work mode, tending to all the details. He was excited at the prospect of leaving the ice and snow behind. He would spend four to five months a year there, then come back to New York for Spring, Summer and Fall. I had a daughter at home and a good job with stability. I couldn't pick up and leave, so I would visit him as often as possible during the months he was away.

We were sitting on Billy's living room couch when

the call came in from the realtor. "Well, Billy, it's yours! They accepted your offer!" His voice carried from Arizona, over the phone, into Billy's New York home, where it danced into our hearts.

We squealed and side-hugged, then the detailed conversation began. As I sat listening, tears welled up in my eyes. I wiped them away. They were persistent little fuckers. I thought I was crying from joy when suddenly I realized, what I was feeling was not joy at all. It was grief. Sadness. Loneliness. "What the hell," I said to myself. I didn't want Billy to see, so I distracted myself with activity.

For two days, I hid it away. He had been talking openly about his fears of the time away from each other. I couldn't say it. I thought I was being weak and if I told him, I would steal his joy and celebration. Eventually, I got grumpy. After lashing out mildly, I took a drive, said a prayer, and realized I needed to share. I am so fortunate he is someone who comes from the same school of thought as me, and who also has deep recovery.

Sometimes in life we talk about our feelings without ill intent or the desire to control other people, and they respond illogically. Many of us grew up that way. So, the process of opening up can be scary. It is a blessing when two people allow one another's feelings but also each take personal accountability.

"Billy, I have to tell you something."

"Okay," he answered in a question.

"I'm really sad. I'm sorry. I want you to do this and I'm really, really happy – for you AND for me. But I'm sad that we'll be apart for large periods of time. I know us. We'll be just fine relationship-wise, but I am going to miss you deeply."

"GOOD," bellowed out from my phone screen.

He knew and he'd just been waiting.

"I'd rather hear that than what I have been hearing," he said.

Up to that point, the Pollyanna side of me was persistently repeating, "We'll be fine. It's fine! Just fine! Don't worry. Fine, fine, fine." Everyone knows that's a load of crap, but I was struggling to get in touch with my fears and feelings. After that we had a great conversation and moved into reality.

"The opposite of dissociation is association," he often says. "You clear up the wreckage of the past, in part, by looking at your feelings today."

He's so right. I need to find the associations – how ignoring my feelings turned into grumpiness and suddenly, my state of being was everyone else's fault. How I was stuffing my emotional needs in fear of disrupting his happiness. How I didn't trust him to support me – not because that was unlikely. In fact, he always supports me emotionally ; but because

91

people in the past could not and that conditioned me.

How my tendency is to run from big feelings. How fear of aloneness drives me to isolate, magnifying the aloneness instead of taking me out of it. I learned all of these behaviors early on when I had no personal power; but that's not me today. So, I associate and the dissociation starts to go away.

So many times, it's just a matter of talking; but not just to anyone – to the right people who have something you want emotionally, who themselves are emotionally mature, and can support you in getting there. It doesn't mean we drop or lose all the people in our lives who can't be that for us; but we prioritize our recovery.

Some people, no matter how hard you try, are going to keep on violating your boundaries. They're going to overreact to your feelings. They're going to dismiss you or always put themselves first. Others have the emotional capacity to stand firm in their values, but also be there for you.

Billy calls it the shelf system. You have to figure out who the people are in your life who help you be the MOST you. They are the one's and two's. There are eight more shelves and you get to decide where people are categorized. It's not an ugly judgement or a way to hide. It's simply learning boundaries.

My spirit is me and my spirit has the right to boundaries. Recovery is learning where the line is and advocating for myself, but also being open and listening. We do it so easily for our children and our loved ones, but so rarely do it for our own little kid inside. I don't want to run anymore.

I don't want to hide. Instead, I take stock of my mental state and I decide. I'm not powerless. I know myself. I'm not always right, but I'm willing to grow. Being in that place in life now is and of itself worthy of all my gratitude, but it's not the only thing. Recovery brings the right people into your life, whether in the form of friendships, acquaintances, or love relationships.

CHILDLIKE DELIGHT

I remember flashes of kindergarten but first grade was epic. I sat in my seat, a name plate at the front of my desk on the first day that read Pamela. The little manager in me loved school so much I ached for it. School clothes shopping was fun, but when I got to walk down the supply aisle at Hills Department Store in the Olean Center Mall, I felt wild inside. Pens. Paper. Folders. Pencils. Erasers. A zip-up pouch.

Most importantly, though, was the Trapper Keeper. I could spend an hour looking through every single option and deciding which one. Lime green borders outlining three adorable puppies. It was going to be a good year.

As always, I settled in, lifted up the top of my desk, and organized the storage space inside. I placed my Trapper Keeper and a pencil on top. I made mental note of the location of the pencil sharpener on the wall and watched the teacher closely for clues of her personality. Then I looked around the room to scan the crew. That's when I made eye contact with Christine.

She smiled triumphantly. I immediately loved her. We made fast best friends and it wasn't long before we were having sleep overs and playing on the same softball team. I couldn't wait to see her in the morning and our outings were the highlight of my life. When Billy talks about his childhood besties he says it's like a countdown. You are sad when you leave them and every moment in between, you are just waiting to have fun again.

Adulthood too often strips us of that childlike delight. Why do we give up childish things? The definition of childish is silly and immature. That's wrong. I think childish should mean happy and eager, excited and free. If you could tap into the feeling you had as a kid when you and your BFF's were the only people in the universe, I think it would far surpass the surface level, draining conversations we too often have as adults.

That's yet another thing recovery has given back to me. I have a bestie. We laugh hysterically. We go do things. We play hard and we talk deeply, like Gordie Lachance and Chris Chambers in Stand By Me. My number one bestie is Billy. He has a profound gift to see my little kid inside. Early on we exchanged pictures of each other as children. Me, all blonde-haired and blue-eyed; my chin resting with curled up hands on either side. Him, head tipped back wearing a black cap, looking straight into the camera.

I remember all the times he just walked with me, when a pile of stressors made a mess of my emotions, like kids so often do for each other. He knows when to wait for me to open up; and often leads me into activities that engage my child inside to counteract the thing I'm struggling with.

Four hours on the golf course on a warm summer day or a half day Harley ride through the country side can put my head in a totally different place. I'm still learning how to give that gift back to him when he's down or grumpy. I was so used to taking it personally, because I had to. Back then, those behaviors were a clue of what was coming next. Being hyper-vigilant was a survival mechanism.

I don't have to do that anymore.

I have other great friends too. I've met some of the absolute coolest human beings on this journey. We go to concerts, conventions, and on Harley rides. We do service together. We laugh loud. We celebrate each other's beauty. I love my people. We are walking this road together through tears and struggles and victories.

Humans need humans. It's just the way it is. I want

humans in my life who are pursuing their best self just as I search out the best in me.

MAGICAL THINGS

*Recovery is like a massively engineered project.
You don't hop on the John Deere and knock out
an acre. You mow the lawn by plucking one
blade of grass at a time. But ya know, time flies
by. You look back at the beauty of the ride and
realize, it was worth every stride.*

The group sits around the perimeter of the room, faces warm and smiling. We span the spectrum of age from hairs of grey to porcelain faces. Love blooms here, which is a miracle. We are an unlikely combination.

In my study and teaching, I was introduced to the Social Change Model for Leadership Development, created by a think tank at UCLA in the 1990's. I came to understand the importance of and difference between individual and shared values. Anytime you bring a group together for a purpose, all the participants bring in their own values. Some of those values can be in conflict. In a group, however, there are inherent shared values based on the group purpose. When a group can clarify and adopt the shared values, it can thrive.

That requires each member to also understand they have certain values that sit outside the group purpose, to personally live those values, but not necessarily demand they be integrated into this activity. It also requires them to respect the differences between one another. If someone cannot live with that dynamic, they have the option to leave the group and find something more fitting.

This has been my experience in recovery. The most sensitive divider among people is often faith; yet I found a place where it's okay to love one another regardless of what you believe. We keep it simple. I accept you and you accept me.

So, if you want to do spells in your room or call on mystic powers by the light of the moon, do it dude. And if I believe a guy in the Middle East wearing Birkenstocks and a dirty robe was the spirit of God in human form, cool for me. The awesome thing is, we can talk about it respectfully.

I have other beliefs too. Grandma Helen was all of four-foot-three – a sturdy German woman who survived atrocity. She was a gifted real estate broker who penned beautiful poetry. She played piano and had an eye for interior decorating. My Grandma was also an incredible psychic, as is one of my childhood best friends David.

For some reason as a society we see this big chasm between psychics and Christianity, but the Bible is full of other-worldly experiences. Burning bushes that talked. Angels visiting humans. People speaking foreign languages they never learned. The dead rising from the grave. In churches today, people speak prophecies and that's okay. Grandma and David both had beautiful faith and special abilities.

She sat at her small kitchen table at the age of 83, light pouring in the window. An old stove furnace stood along the wall with a pot of water on top. She spread the cards out before her. They were antique – likely from the 1920's. She grew up in the oil fields of Pennsylvania and had visions as a little girl. One afternoon, a wagon came down the old dirt road and she ran after it. A group of gypsies, with all their belongings in the back, filled its seats. They saw her coming. The gentleman driving stepped down to the ground and held out his hand.

"You have a gift," he said quietly.

"What do you mean," the little girl asked.

"You can see things," he responded.

He handed her a deck of hand-drawn cards and went on his way. She had them to the day she died. An original tarot, they were dark green with black markings. When she spread them out on the table, she'd inhale deeply and close her eyes. When she spoke, it resembled healing.

As a little girl it scared me. Later she told me some things I refused to believe and it angered me. Eventually, I saw what it really was. She was a woman of deep faith and the readings were a connection her spirit made with the spirit in all things. I like to reconcile that with my faith. God doesn't live in a box to me.

Despite all the painful and awful experiences that I needed to grieve from my growing up years, there were so many magical things, like Grandma and David.

LOVE

The pen leaves blue lines in the form of words on ivory paper that smells of wood. I write the entry that marks the end of one journey and the beginning of another. Writing is my healing process. All these pages and all these years are how I found Pammy; how I learned to truly love myself.

This recovery has taught me to let go of suffering, grow in my understanding, and celebrate the good that grew in me. My faith these days is an easy and soft kind of faith. It's not a superpower. I'm human. In fact, it takes none of my pain away. For me, it sits somewhere between fate and practicality.

Fate says nothing is up to me. Practicality says everything is within my power to achieve. Neither one has proven true for me, and my life is the only proof I need. If I believed fate was all there was, I would either end up hating God and people or feeling like a touched human being – special; above others. If I rely only on practicality, I leave no room for the ways life moves us around – the unexpected; the out of my control.

While I have a super easy belief that comes naturally to me, others like Billy gravitate between agnosticism and a spirit-centered belief. He and I came to the conclusion one afternoon, God isn't a vending machine. We don't get what want, often times. In fact, we may not even get what we need. Some of us pray for a parking place closer to the front door. Others say "fuck God, I don't need that guy."

Maybe, just maybe, God or whatever you want to call it is felt most powerfully when that spirit connects with our own true spirit inside. That means we have to know ourselves deeply. We have set our spirit free.

Life can be beautiful and life can be absolutely awful. We're really just along for the ride. Serenity comes when I give up to it, try to do the right things, and ask for relief from the source of all peace.

Even writing all this, I imagine the myriad reactions – like when people post something on social media and everybody responds so passionately trying to dissuade them or change their mind. Some make it their life's mission to discredit everything they said – to attach judgements to it. We will be judged by others. That's a simple fact.

Fortunately, someone told me I don't have to be

understood to be happy. In fact, prepare to be mis-
understood. Now that is revolutionary! I spent a
lifetime wholly dependent on others for feelings of
intimacy, approval, affection, direction, and a sense
of self-worth. Taking any of those away was devas-
tating. Not today.

Like a baby tentatively letting go of her mother's
hands to take her first glorious steps, I release de-
pendence. I wobble forward, lifting one leg ever so
slowly, holding steady by straightening my arms. I
move an inch then plant that foot firmly on the
ground before picking up the other. I still look for
good, healthy counsel – like the baby occasionally
touching her mother's hand.

When you love yourself, you can accept love from
others. You can receive non-controlling, non-sham-
ing direction without clinging to it like a life pre-
server. Learning to not need approval magnifies
the kind of self-worth that emanates from the inside out. Instead of fearing relationships or grasping
them with crushing hands, you enjoy them the way
you let the wind tickle your skin. I've said it before
and I'll say it again – it's not just me.

I've watched tensed up, stressed out, cut-off older
teens finally find out they have ADHD after a lifetime of being shamed for behaviors they didn't
understand, and instantly turn into goofy kids
again. I've watched adults in their 50's and 60's tell
their childhood story for the first time in their life

and allow themselves to feel like they should have felt when they were 13. They adopted a glow immediately. I've seen someone who never smiled, walk the long, slow road to recovering his true self, and soon adopt a grin so attractive it set the room afire.

Look, we are all special, and if you think I'm soft for saying so, I really don't care. Each and every one of us has something truly unique to share. That something is YOU.

There is only one of you. Your voice, your physical presence on earth, your personality, your spirit, your gifts and abilities – they make up you. That is not for anyone else to shape or groom. They can contribute, buy <u>you</u> must define you.

So, go in deep. Look at all the things that made you, you. The good. The bad. The in-between. Don't let fear or shame stop you. Elicit help when you need to.

I still do. And every day I wake up grateful. That is a gift I'll never trade.

Until We Meet Again...

> Bless my journey, spirit of all things. I thank
> you for that which is unending.

> May the life inside me emanate free, like my
> lover's face staring back at me;

> Like the mountain and the sunset; the grass
> between my toes;

> The sunshine on the ocean; a baby's button
> nose.

> Help me cling to "childish" things; embrace
> your sense of innocense -

> A puppy, a fish, a dandelion wish, the deep
> blue sea and outer space.

> The ups and downs, they come and go. Heal-
> ing is not for the faint of heart,

> but there is a hand that never let's go. It has
> been inside me from the very start.

May all the blessings of freedom be yours
~Pam

Made in the USA
Las Vegas, NV
10 October 2021

32090612R00065